TENNIS

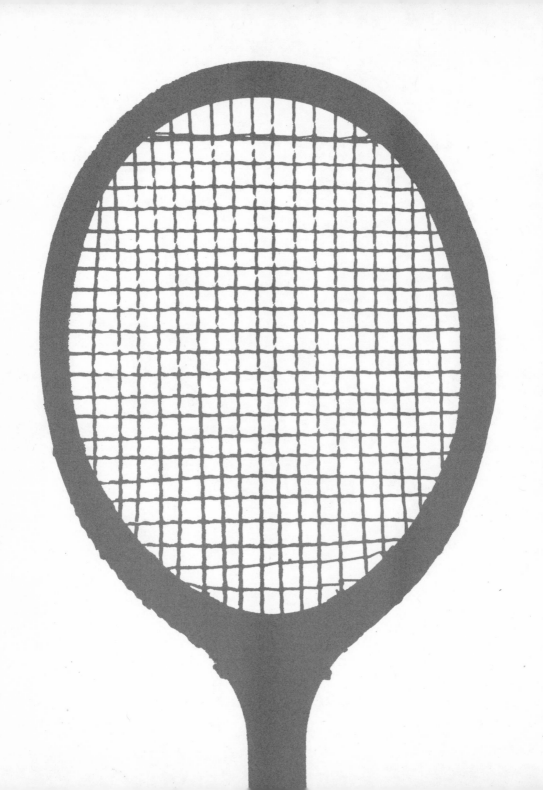

tennis

by Bill McCormick

FRANKLIN WATTS, INC. | NEW YORK | 1973

←A FIRST BOOK→

Cover design by One + One Studio

Phctographs courtesy of:
Australian News and Information Bureau: p. 46; The New York
Public Library Picture Collection: pp. vi, 4, 15, 56 (left), 60
(top left); U.S.L.T.A.: pp. 10, 18, 23, 26, 29, 32, 36, 39, 42, 51,
56 (right), 58 (left and right), 60 (bottom left and right), 61

Library of Congress Cataloging in Publication Data

McCormick, Bill.
    Tennis.
    (A First book)
    SUMMARY: Discusses the origins of tennis, its equip-
ment, rules, scoring, and plays and includes a brief descrip-
tion of some tennis "greats."
    1. Tennis—Juvenile literature. [1. Tennis] I. Title.
GV995.M15   796.34'2   73-3407
ISBN 0-531-00803-7

24270

CONTENTS

THE GAME OF A LIFETIME

Tennis is the game of a lifetime, a participation sport to grow up with and grow old with.

Tennis enjoys such worldwide popularity that facilities are available almost everywhere, even in the most out-of-the-way places. For those without access to school, club, or private tennis courts, there are public courts in all cities and in practically every town and village.

Because tennis is so widely played, there is no lack of good competition or playing partners on every level of competence wherever you go. Indeed, tennis is such a universal sport that the entry list for the All-England Championships at Wimbledon each year reads like the roster of the United Nations; and great players from all over the world come in all sizes, shapes, and colors.

Tennis is a comparatively inexpensive sport. Court fees, where required, are usually quite reasonable. Rackets vary widely in price from only a few dollars to not much more than the cost of one or two golf clubs. The best of tennis shoes are less expensive than the cheapest of ordinary footwear. Tennis balls are inexpensive, do not wear out rapidly, and do not get lost as easily as golf balls.

Those concerned with the physical fitness of the nation strongly urge every youth to take up some sport that will last a lifetime, providing not only recreation but also healthful exercise from childhood through old age. Tennis is ideal for this purpose. Championship

1

competitive tennis is one of the most strenuous of all sports, but the social game is played according to physical ability, age, and other factors that must be taken into consideration when choosing a lifetime sport.

THE ORIGINS OF TENNIS

Modern tennis probably developed from handball games played by the Arabs and Egyptians as early as 500 B.C., although some historians believe it started with competition between Greeks and Romans in later centuries. Handball became particularly popular in France, where players adopted gloves and later paddles to avoid stinging their hands. These paddles eventually evolved into the modern tennis racket.

Over the years, handball played with paddles became known as court tennis; it was played in a walled court, with the ball playable off side and end walls as well as from the floor. Court tennis was popular with the aristocracy and many of the monarchs of France and England were devotees, including King Henry II of France and Britain's vigorous Henry VIII. Tennis is still very popular in France, a country that has produced many modern champions.

Tennis as it is played today was introduced by a British army major named Walter Clopton Wingfield, who tried to patent the pastime. In 1873 he wrote a book, *Sphairistike or Lawn Tennis* (the derivation and meaning of the word "Sphairistike" are not clear), and he demonstrated the game at a lawn party in Wales. The Marlyebone Cricket Club arranged an exhibition of the game at their Lord's cricket affair in 1875. That same year the sport was introduced to the All-England Croquet Club at Wimbledon, which staged its first lawn tennis championship in 1877. Today the All-

3

LE IEV
ROYAL DE
LA PAVLME.

A PARIS
Chez Charles Hulpeau

England Championships for men and women, still contested on the same Wimbledon site in greater London, offer the sport's most highly prized titles.

The British took tennis to every nook and cranny of their far-flung empire, but it was a young woman returning from a vacation in Bermuda who brought the pastime to America in 1874. United States customs authorities had never seen anything like the strange paraphernalia of the game she brought with her, so they held up entry of the rackets and balls while they tried to figure out how to tax them. They finally surrendered and admitted the equipment free of import duty.

By 1881 tennis had become so popular in America that the United States Lawn Tennis Association was organized to set standard rules and conditions of play. After many years, the U.S.L.T.A. relaxed their rules to permit amateurs to compete against professionals, as in golf. This has added tremendous interest to the big tournaments and stimulated thousands of young people to learn the game.

Court tennis
being played in
Paris, France,
about 1623.

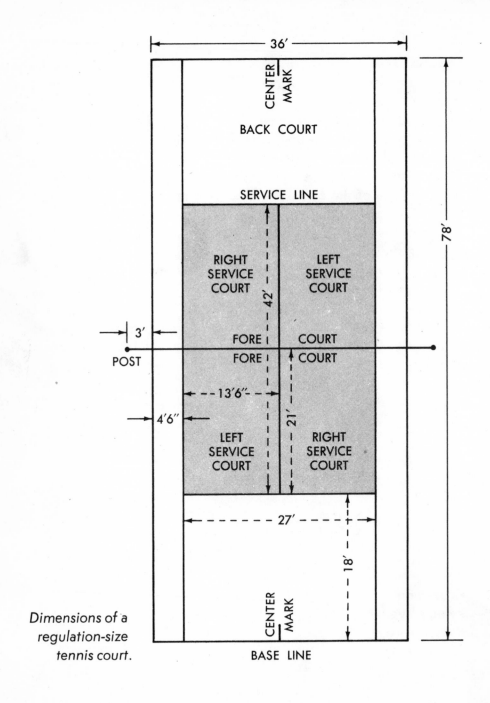

Dimensions of a regulation-size tennis court.

THE COURT

Modern tennis is played either on grass or lawn courts — which are difficult to maintain — or, more usually in the United States, on clay, asphalt, cement, or some other suitable surface. The rules of the game are the same no matter which kind of surface is used.

All courts are laid out so that either singles matches (one player on each side of the net) or doubles (two players on each side) can be played on them. Singles and doubles courts are identical except that separate sidelines make the doubles playing surface 36 feet wide instead of the 27 feet used in singles.

The court is 78 feet long overall and the length is divided in half by the net, which stands 3 feet high in the middle and about 3½ feet at the end posts.

The forecourt runs 21 feet from the net back to the court's end (the baseline) on each side of the net. Each court is divided by a line down its middle, thus breaking each forecourt into two sections measuring 21 feet by 13½ feet for singles and doubles. These are called the left and right service courts and it is into them that the ball must be placed on each fair service. The area behind the service courts is called the backcourt.

The 4½-foot by 78-foot areas, which flank either end of the court perpendicular to the net, form the boundaries for doubles play (except the service, which must be in the same 21-foot by 13½-foot area that is used for singles service).

THE GAME

The basic object of the game is to knock a ball back and forth across the net into the playing area, until one player loses a point by hitting the ball either out of the playing area or into the net.

The aim of each player is to hit the ball into the opponent's court so that it is out of his reach or he returns the ball out of bounds or sends it into the net.

Play begins with the server hitting the ball — that is, serving it — diagonally from behind the baseline so that it lands beyond the net in the opposite service court. One player serves an entire game and is given two service tries each time the ball is put into play. The serve changes hands after each game. A "let" ball — one that caroms off the top of the net into the proper service court — is considered neither as a fair ball nor a faulty serve and entitles the server to another try. A served ball may be hit and returned only after the first bounce, and before the second, from the service court. If it lands outside the service court it is considered a fault. A server making two faults loses the point. Stepping over the baseline on the serve is also considered a fault; however, one foot may go over the baseline before the ball is struck, provided it does not touch the line or the court surface.

First serve in a game is always from behind the baseline in that half of the court on the server's right. Service then is alternated from side to side after each point is scored.

After the first game, the players change sides of the net. From then on they change after every two games, or after odd numbered games, until their match is finished.

Once the serve is completed, the ball may be hit into the entire area of the opponent's court until a point is scored (a ball that hits the line in an opponent's court is considered fair). The ball may be hit either before it hits the playing surface or after the first bounce — but always before it hits the court's surface a second time. A ball may also strike the net and be considered fairly returned only if it falls into the opponent's court.

To summarize, points are lost by a player who (1) commits two service faults; (2) fails to return to the opponent's court a ball that has been hit fairly into his court; (3) hits a ball into the net; or (4) hits a ball out of the opponent's court.

Margaret Court (right, with cup),
winning in two sets at
Forest Hills, New York.
Nancy Richey stands at left.

SCORING

The origin of the rather peculiar method of scoring in tennis is obscure, but it is generally agreed that the term "love," signifying "no score," is a corruption of the French term "l'oeuf," (pronounced "luff"), meaning the egg, or zero. Other than that, tennis scoring is inexplicable, but easy enough to understand.

The first two points scored by a player count 15 each, the third counts 10. Thus, a player making three consecutive points would have his score recorded as 15-30-40. If that player again makes a point he wins the game, unless his opponent also has made three points and the score is tied. In that case, the score is called "deuce" instead of 40-40 or 40-all. From then on a player has to make two consecutive points to win the game.

A player scoring one point after deuce is said to have the advantage, or "ad." If he fails to score the next point, the score returns to deuce.

The term love is always used to designate a zero score. In announcing scores, the server's score always is announced first. Thus, the announcement of a 15-40 score indicates that the server has made one point, his opponent three. The announcement "40-love" means that the server has made three points, the receiver none.

A set consists of six games or more. The first player to take six games wins the set, if the opponent has won no more than four games. If the players are tied at 4-all or 5-all, one player must win two consecutive games to win the set.

In men's tournament play, the best three out of five sets wins a match. Women's matches are usually played with two out of three sets winning the match. These conditions may be changed by local tournament authorities and are usually amended for social play.

EQUIPMENT

The only equipment a player really needs is tennis shoes, balls, and a racket. There are other accessories that may make the game more enjoyable, but they are not essential.

Most tennis shoes have grooved soles. These are excellent for play on composition or cement courts because they provide good traction on very hard surfaces. On grass or clay courts, relatively smooth soles that do not damage the surface are more suitable. In fact, shoes with grooved soles are strictly forbidden on some grass and clay courts.

It is advisable to wear woolen socks to absorb perspiration and to avoid blisters. If your feet tend to blister easily, a pair of thin socks may be worn under the woolen ones. White socks are preferable, not only because white is the traditional color of tennis garb, but also because they are less prone to infect open blisters.

The racket with which the ball is hit is ordinarily about 27 inches long, and has a wooden or metal frame supporting a hitting surface of tightly strung threads of heavy, resilient fiber. The proper size of the racket depends entirely upon the physical capabilities of the player who will use it. It is advisable that a beginner not select a racket that is too heavy to be swung easily. Indeed rackets that are too heavy are the primary cause of many cases of so-called "tennis elbow" and sore arms.

Standard rackets for men weigh as much as 14½ ounces or more

(Don Budge, a tennis champion in the late 1930s, employed one that weighed 16 ounces). Standard women's rackets usually weigh no more than 14¼ ounces.

The table below shows the approximate weight and grip circumference ordinarily recommended for beginners of various ages.

AGE	WEIGHT	HANDLE
8-9 (boys & girls)	12 oz.	4¼ in.
10-12 (boys)	12½-13 oz.	4¼-4½ in.
10-12 (girls)	12½-13 oz.	4¼ in.
13-14 (boys)	13¼-13¾ oz.	4½-4⅝ in.
13-14 (girls)	12¾-13 oz.	4⅜-4½ in.

A beginner with great wrist strength and large hands probably would want a heavier racket with a larger grip than the one suggested for his or her age group. A less strong novice with small hands might want a lighter racket with a smaller grip.

Beginners, who will be returning the ball largely from the back court rather than at the net, are advised to purchase a racket that is slightly heavy in the head so that it will do most of the work when they stroke.

Care should be taken not to purchase a racket with too small a handle, since this could cause the racket to twist in the hand, particularly on a groundstroke.

The best thing is to try rackets of different weights and handle sizes until you find one that feels right for you — one that seems to be an extension of your arm and that can be swung freely and easily.

Althea Gibson, one of the all-time greats of tennis, in tournament attire at Forest Hills.

Nylon strings are best for general use. They are less expensive than gut strings, last longer, and resist dampness better. However, they do not propel the ball with the speed and spin that are part of every good player's game.

The ball is unstitched, felt-covered, inflated rubber about 2½ inches in diameter. New or slightly used tennis balls bounce better and fly straighter than those that are worn, because the fuzz on them keeps them in reasonably predictable flight.

There are a few simple accessory pieces of equipment that may prove useful, although they are not essential. For players with excessively sweaty hands there are terry cloth grips, which may be fitted over the racket's regular handle. A racket press prevents the frame from warping, and a racket case will protect the strings from dampness. Sweatbands of various materials may be purchased to wear around the head to prevent perspiration from dripping onto the face or the lenses of glasses. There are also available elasticized cloth bands that fit snugly around the wrists to absorb perspiration which might otherwise dribble onto the handle, interfering with the player's grasp on the racket.

While not mandatory, white is traditionally worn on the tennis court, probably because it tends to be heat resistant. Clothing should be loose enough to be comfortable and allow complete freedom of movement.

TENNIS DEMANDS AND ATTITUDES

Tennis is a game that makes demands upon all of a player's resources, both mental and physical. Physically, tennis calls for fine coordination, speed, power, and stamina. Mentally, the game calls for determination, intense concentration, and the ability to anticipate and outwit an opponent. It is with good reason that tennis has been called "chess with muscles."

Actually, tennis is not nearly as formidable as it sounds — for one good reason. No one player has yet developed all his tennis resources to perfection. Every player has his weaknesses, even the great champions who dazzle Forest Hills and Wimbledon with their brilliant performances. A player with a smashing serve and good forehand may have a weak backhand. One with a devastating backhand and smash could suffer from an erratic serve and inaccurate placement shots.

In addition, a player with all the shots at his physical beck and call may be slow of reflex and unable to cope with puzzling changes of pace and confusing tactics. By learning to take advantage of their own strong points and capitalize on an opponent's weaknesses, all players can improve their game.

Tennis is a lonely game, a game of self-reliance. On the court — at least in singles — there is no one to turn to for help, no one to blame for defeat but yourself.

At its best, tennis can also be savagely ruthless. It is a competition

*Rod Laver, winner of the
Grand Slam of tennis in 1961,
using his famous left hand.*

in which it is not considered unsportsmanlike to attack an opponent relentlessly at his weakest point and overwhelm him with your own strengths.

If an opponent is out of condition, it is not only perfectly proper, but good tennis to keep him running ragged — from forecourt to backcourt, from side to side — until he can be defeated. Against a player who tends to send returns into the net or out of the court, it is good tactics to concentrate on keeping the ball in play until he himself makes an error. Study of even the very best players shows that they lose more points on their own errors than they do by missing an opponent's shots.

An opponent with the right attitude toward the game will not resent such tactics employed against him. Rather, he will welcome them, because they serve to point up his weaknesses and indicate those areas in which his game should be improved.

Rod Laver, who won the Grand Slam of tennis (the Australian, French, All-England, and American singles championships) in 1961, is from Australia, where tennis enthusiasts place great stress on physical conditioning and merciless attack. Laver has high regard for Charlie Hollis, the man who taught him the game, even though — as Laver admits — Hollis was a relentless coach. Hollis repeatedly sent young Laver into competition that was too stiff to imbue him with "killer instinct" and Hollis himself administered defeat after defeat to his pupil for four years to emphasize weaknesses that needed correction.

"I didn't beat Charlie for the first time until I was 14," recalls Laver.

Those four years of pounding instruction by a teacher, who was a second father to him, did perhaps as much as anything else to fashion Rod Laver into a great champion.

The first lesson every good instructor teaches every tennis pupil — and the one Hollis taught Laver at the beginning of their long association — is to . . .

SHAKE HANDS WITH THE RACKET

There is no standard way of holding the racket that is suitable for all types of shots. However, even though there are some other grips, the one known as the Eastern grip is the most generally useful and it can be adjusted for just about every known situation and stroke.

The Eastern grip is quite easy and natural. The player holds the racket by the throat in his left hand, with the handle pointing toward his body, the face of the racket perpendicular to the ground. Then he shakes hands with the racket at the end of the handle with his right hand (or left hand, if he is left-handed).

The index finger is extended along the handle as though it were about to pull the trigger on a gun. The thumb rests against the end of the middle finger and the "V" formed by the fingers and thumb points straight down the top of the handle toward the head. The palm of the hand should be in back of the handle, with the back of the hand parallel to the face of the racket (see page 21).

Variations of the Eastern grip necessary to adapt to the various basic tennis strokes will be explained as the shots themselves are discussed.

Although it has been employed with success by some good players, the unorthodox two-handed grip is not favored by most instructors because it reduces the reach.

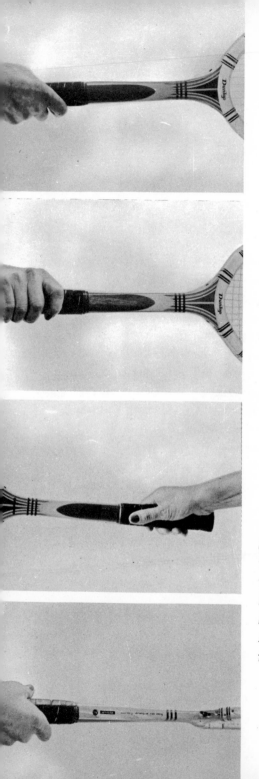

From top: the Eastern
forehand grip; a front
view of the Eastern
backhand grip; the
Eastern backhand grip
seen from the back;
the Continental grip.

PLAY!

For many years, beginners who were naturally left-handed were urged by instructors to learn to play right-handed. Now it is conceded that southpaws and right-handers can employ exactly the same playing techniques and that, in fact, left-handers have a slight advantage over those who hold the racket in the right hand. In the following instructions, which are given for right-handers, southpaws should merely substitute left for right and vice versa.

The best way to begin to learn to play is to hit the ball back and forth over the net with someone. Do not worry about where the ball lands. Until you get the complete feel of the racket, just keep hitting it back and forth as many times as you can without sending it into the net. If you cannot find someone to rally with you, as they say in tennis, bounce the ball against a backdrop or a wall, hitting it back about net high.

The position for rallying is usually assumed by standing near the center of the court close to the baseline, with the weight on the balls of the feet and knees slightly bent. In this way, the player can take off toward the ball no matter where it lands.

The American tennis star
Arthur Ashe
at the rallying position.

When you are in the ready position, the racket should be supported mainly by the left hand holding it at the throat, pointing toward the net. The right hand should grip the handle lightly, since the left controls the racket as it is moved to the right or left in preparation for a forehand or backhand return. Most good players firm up their grip just before they begin the stroke, leaving them an option on how to hit their return until the last split second.

If the ball comes over the net to the player's right, a forehand return is indicated.

THE FOREHAND

In the ready position, watch the ball closely as your opponent hits it. You must decide instantaneously where the ball will hit and bounce, and then move speedily into position to stroke the return. Your arm must be almost fully extended as you make the swing, since the arm should be straight, never bent, when hitting any orthodox shot.

As you move in to get set for the return, draw the racket back horizontally, so you will not have to do it at the last second. When in position to stroke the ball, your weight will be on the right foot, which should be parallel to the baseline and net. The feet should be about 1½ feet apart, with the left foot about 6 inches closer to the right sideline than the right, at about a 45 degree angle to the net. The left side of the body should point toward the net and the racket should be drawn back at about a right angle to the baseline.

Ordinarily, the best time to start the hitting-through movement on the ball is when the ball is about 2 feet from your left foot. The racket is kept perpendicular to the ground and the shoulders and hips turn to the left as you meet the ball squarely with the racket about waist high. During the sweep-through motion, weight shifts to the left foot. Elbows are slightly bent at impact and the grip should be firm. A properly hit forehand will have a "follow through," in which the racket is propelled in a straight line toward the target for a brief period, rather than whipping immediately around the body. Hit through the ball, do not chop at it. 25

If the ball arrives at the point of impact lower than you had anticipated when you took your stroking stance, do not drop the head of the racket to hit the ball. Instead, bend your knees in order to make proper contact.

A properly stroked ball will have topspin from the forehand. Topspin makes the ball take a nose-dive after it has gone over the net and come out of the bounce low. Only the experts attempt to apply extra spin by turning the wrists.

Concentration is most important. Keep your eye, and mind, on the ball until after it is well hit, no matter how strong the temptation to look over the net to see if the ball is going where you aimed it or how well your opponent is set to return it fairly. After the ball is well on its way, get set for the return, which will probably come quicker than you can say Billie Jean King.

After the novice has gained confidence that his forehand shots will clear the net, he can practice keeping them in fair territory. After that, he can practice placing the ball where it will prove the most embarrassing to an opponent. To send the ball down the middle of the court, aim for the middle of the net. To attack an opponent's backhand, hit the ball a split second late. To present him with a forehand return, hit the ball a little early.

Only practice can teach the novice how late or how early to hit the ball to obtain the desired results, for in tennis, practice is the name of the game.

Billie Jean King
retrieving with
a forehand shot.

THE BACKHAND

For no good reason, most beginners in tennis seem to fear the backhand. Actually, the backhand stroke is easier than the forehand because the body is out of the way, allowing a more natural, less impeded swing than the forehand.

A player without a backhand is not even half a player. Running around the ball to avoid playing a backhand is the worst thing a novice can do. It is not only generally futile, it is tiring and opens up vast areas of your court to counterattack. A player who keeps running around the ball or jabbing at it ineffectually not only loses points, he never develops a decent backhand.

The backhand is played with a variation of the Eastern forehand grip, which usually is called the Eastern backhand grip. This grip is taken by assuming the Eastern forehand grip and twisting the racket slightly so that the palm of the hand is on top of the handle (instead of behind it) and the "V" formed by the index finger and the thumb lies on the upper left bevel of the handle. Instead of being in the "trigger pulling" position of the Eastern forehand grip, the index finger should be curved around the handle. The thumb

*Classic backhand form
is shown here by
Tony Roche at the
moment of backswing.*

28

can either be placed against the index finger or along the length of the bevel, whichever feels more comfortable and seems to give better control (see page 21).

To get ready for the backhand return, move the racket back with your left hand on the throat, turning the shoulders to the left in the same motion. When you are in position, the left foot, which bears your weight, will be behind your body and the right foot ahead of the body, about 2 feet to the left of your right foot. Both knees should be bent slightly, the racket parallel to the net and about waist high.

The backhand is a sweeping motion in which the racket moves from right to left parallel to the ground until it meets the ball with its face perpendicular to the ground. Weight shifts to the right foot and the racket should rise slightly at and after impact.

Backspin, which causes the ball to bounce with a lift, is imparted naturally by the backhand and the novice should not strive for additional spin by purposely working the wrists.

The routine for practicing the backhand is the same as for the forehand — rallying across the net with a partner or bouncing the ball off a wall until the stroke feels natural without regard to placement. When you have mastered this, then try to keep the ball in a fair area and send it where your opponent is not.

THE SERVE

Many players consider the serve the most important shot in tennis. The serving player has an advantage over the receiver, both strategically and psychologically.

A player with a good serve can set the pace and determine to a large degree how the play shall go until a point is scored. The serve is also the one shot in which a player — the server — has complete control of the ball. The receiver has nothing whatsoever to do with the serve except to wait and try to return it fairly.

Good tournament players win the games they serve with monotonous regularity. Breaking service — that is, winning a game against the server — is the aim of every good player because it usually gives the winner an edge over his opponent that takes him well toward victory in the set.

The most common fault in serving is to throw away the first serve (since two tries are allowed) by striving for an ace (an unreturnable ball) on the first try. Such a maneuver must necessarily be followed by a serve that does little more than land fair in the opponent's court, and the server runs the grave risk of losing the point. Not only that, continual double serves are physically tiring to the server.

A player should try to make at least 50 percent of his first serves fair, serving the first ball against his opponent's weaknesses, rather than striving to "cannonball" it over the net.

The slice serve is the only standard way of putting the ball into

31

play that is recommended for the novice. The American twist and flat service (or cannonball) are only for more advanced players.

The slice serve is fairly easy to control and once it is mastered is a most consistent and serviceable method of putting the ball into play.

The Continental grip is the most satisfactory for the slice serve. In this grip, the palm rests over the upper right bevel of the handle instead of behind the face of the racket. The index finger is extended along the handle and the thumb lies flat against the flat side of the handle. This grip makes for better wrist control, which is essential in the slice serve (see page 21).

The first serve in a game is always made to the deuce, or first court, which is on the server's left, and the receiver's right. When in position to serve the slice serve to the deuce court, the body is sideways to the net, the left foot an inch or so behind the baseline and as near as possible to the center marker at about a 45 degree angle to the net. The right foot is about 18 inches or so behind and about 6 inches to the right of the left foot, parallel to the sideline. Weight is evenly distributed. The racket is held about waist high with its head slightly elevated and about a foot away from the left hip. The ball is held in the left hand against the strings of the racket.

The movements for the toss — to get the ball into the air to be hit — and the backswing start simultaneously with a shift of body weight to the right foot. As the left hand tosses the ball into the air, the right arm — with bent elbow — brings the racket up and over the right shoulder until the head of the racket is horizontal and about opposite the right cheek. As the ball reaches the apex of the toss, the right arm and shoulder move forward and the right arm is ex-

Excellent serving form
is shown here
by Billie Jean King.

tended to give full sweep to the stroke. Simultaneously, the left arm moves down and the body twists to the left as weight is transferred from the right to the left foot. As the ball is hit, the wrist should snap down and forward to impart extra sidespin.

Service to the ad, or second, court — the one on the server's right, receiver's left — can be made farther away from the center marker to enable the ball to be played to the receiver's backhand. The actual stroking of the ball is done exactly the same as service to the deuce court.

Putting all the elements of the serve together is something that can be accomplished only by practice and more practice. The most important element is the toss. If it is not made so that the ball is in precisely the right place at the right time to be properly stroked, the serve cannot be effective. Great champions have spent months practicing just the toss until they were satisfied.

THE VOLLEY

To volley is to return the ball before it touches the ground instead of waiting for it to bounce. Volleying, especially from close to the net, is one of the most effective ways to attack an opponent and take the initiative from him. A well-timed volley can catch an opponent off balance by not giving him time to get set for a return. If an opponent realizes you can volley well, he will tend to hit the ball deep on returns to keep you from coming to the net. The law of averages dictates that the more deep returns there are, the more chance there is of one of them going out of the court.

The volley is best stroked with the Eastern backhand grip. Position for the volley preferably should be taken about 6 feet from the net. Weight is on the balls of the feet, knees slightly flexed, ready to move to either side. The racket is held in front of the player, head tilted upward, also ready to move to right or left as required. The ball is stroked from a comparatively short backswing, when it is about 2 feet away from the player, with the racket head always held higher than the wrist.

The volley is a stroke, not a punch, but with far less follow-through than a groundstroke. The shortened swing allows more time to get into position for the return and to leave the net if the ball is driven or lobbed deep into the player's court.

THE LOB

A lob is a stroke in which the racket comes under the ball, sending it high. It is a most useful shot and can be employed for both attack and defense.

To a novice, the principal use of the lob is defensive. He employs it to return balls that he is unable to get set to return with a groundstroke or volley — just to get the ball over the net and have time to reorganize himself. The lob may also be used defensively to return a ball into deep territory near the sidelines, which has drawn the returner off balance for the next shot.

Offensively, the lob may be used to run an opponent around the court to tire him, to draw a good volleyer away from the net, or as a change of pace when an opponent seems to be too much in command.

Basically, the lob stroke is the same employed in groundstrokes, except that the ball is hit upward by bringing the racket under it with the face slightly tilted.

A volley shot
by Ilie Nastase,
the Romanian star.

THE SMASH

The smash is a killer shot — the heavy artillery of tennis. It is played for only one purpose; to hit the ball so a player cannot possibly return it or, hopefully, even lay a racket on it. It is the most spectacular and aggressive shot in the game, sending the ball into an opponent's court like a projectile.

The smash looks so deceptively easy that even the best of players are frequently lured into an error. It is not uncommon to see the best players in the world at Wimbledon or Forest Hills slam an apparently sure-kill smash into the net or out of the court, usually as a result of overconfidence.

The smash is delivered most safely and effectively from close to the net. The farther back a player attempts a smash, the less likely it is that it will work.

The Continental grip is used for the smash, which may be hit either before or after the ball has bounced. The smash in execution resembles the serve, with a shorter backswing. It has been described as a serve in which the opponent tosses the ball into position.

The smash also provides a great way to work off steam during a match. Slamming the ball can take a lot of pressure off a player who has been plagued by narrowly missed line shots or balls that, for some perverse reason of their own, barely fail to clear the net.

Yet these are just fringe benefits of the smash; its main purpose is to clearly and decisively score a point.

The beginning of a smash.

POTPOURRI

Tennis is a game of such infinite variety that no player has ever learned all there is to know about it or completely mastered every technique in the potpourri the sport affords. This is one of the great fascinations of tennis.

There is an almost endless catalogue of strokes to be learned — chop shots, spins, half-volleys, cannonball serves, the American twist, drop shots, and so on.

New and intriguing situations arise in almost every match. Each new opponent faced offers a unique and different challenge. There is no permanent strategy. Tactics change from minute to minute.

Thus, tennis becomes a game of instant improvisations and adaptations in strategy and tactics to the ever-changing aspects of the game. There are, however, certain basic maneuvers that the novice can learn at the outset.

SINGLES TACTICS

Some of the basic tactics and strategies of tennis have already been mentioned, such as getting in the first serve, keeping the ball in play to increase the chances of an opponent making an error, and others. But there are more.

Never rely solely on your best shot or shots. Mix them up so that an opponent cannot anticipate what you will do next. This can not only prove disconcerting to an opponent, it can also give you an opportunity to improve your own weak shots, which can be strengthened only by use and practice.

Do not be overconfident, especially with the smash. Even though the ball is sitting up in the air waiting to be knocked down, give this killing shot the same concentration and attention that you would bestow on the most difficult shot.

Attack your opponent's weaknesses. If his backhand is feeble, play to it. If he is slow afoot, keep him moving around the court, never allowing him time to get properly set for the return.

If he tends to "throw away" the first serve, move in on his second serve and be prepared to deal with it decisively.

If an opponent seems ill at ease at the net, try to draw him into it. If he volleys well or his groundstrokes tend to go astray, play him deep so that he cannot volley from the net and runs the risk of errors on his groundstrokes.

If an opponent is prone to misjudge his smashes, lob to him to give him every opportunity to make more such errors.

Learn to relax and concentrate. Good players relax completely while changing sides and between exchanges, but their concentration is turned on full force when the chips are down. Stan Smith, Wimbledon champion of 1972, said, after bearing down on Ilie Nastase, the Rumanian, in one set of a Davis Cup match in Bucharest, "I got a headache from concentrating so hard." Yet, between flurries of hectic activity, Smith appeared completely relaxed and loose.

The American ace Stan Smith,
1972 Wimbledon champion.

DOUBLES

Doubles play involves no special rules except that the court surface is larger; that is, the two alleys, each 4½ feet wide, are used on either side of the court. Doubles teams change sides after each game. One member of a team serves an entire game, rotating service with his partner. Thus, the player who serves the first game, serves the third, the fifth, and so forth. The server serves to the same opponent for an entire game and only the receiver can return a serve. After the serve, either partner on a team can stroke a return. If a player hits a ball, even a slight tick, it cannot be stroked by his partner. However, if a doubles player misses a ball entirely (except on the serve), his partner may stroke it or the player who has missed may take a second swing provided he hits the ball before the second bounce.

DOUBLES TACTICS

Doubles require more play at the net and it is a team game, rather than one of individual effort and self-reliance. This means that not all good singles players make good doubles partners, and vice versa. Two very good singles players may perform badly as a team, either because their games are not compatible — that is, they do not meld as a team — or perhaps because of a clash of personalities. For instance, an aggressive player who is teamed with one who tends to stay on the defensive can coordinate their efforts with splendid results, but this requires complete understanding of the role each is to play.

On a good doubles team, both players will usually strive to get to the net where they can cut off returns with volleys. Less accomplished players usually play one partner deep — ordinarily the server or receiver — while the other partner advances to the net.

Lobbing is more important in doubles than it is in singles, since it can be used to force one or both opponents from the net deep into the court, which is not a strategically sound position in doubles.

Since so much of the play is at or near the net, the smash is of great value in doubles. A lob, of which there are usually more in doubles than in singles, can present an enticing target for a sound smash, especially if the lob is directed near the net.

Good volleying is absolutely essential to good doubles play. The best singles player in the world whose volley is weak will make a poor doubles partner. A player whose volley is a strong point, but who is too deficient in other techniques to be good at singles, may prove to be an excellent doubles partner.

While doubles is, generally speaking, more aggressive than singles, doubles play offers more chance to relax and is less fatiguing because the burden is shared by a partner.

Doubles play becomes more and more popular every day. Not only because it is a fascinating social game, but also because it is often obligatory to team up with another couple on some crowded courts, especially on days when play is particularly heavy.

*A common
doubles strategy.*

TENNIS ETIQUETTE

While tennis as we know it today is popular with people in all countries and in every walk of life, it was the British aristocracy that first took to the modern game. The sport itself has its roots in somewhat similar pastimes that were almost a prerogative of royalty. With such a background, over the years the sport has become imbued with a tradition of manners and customs that might, if it were not such a bad pun, be described as courtly.

No matter how ruthless and relentless the competition, it is always conducted according to a code of conduct almost as demanding as the rules that governed the knights of yore. The traditional courtesy extends even to spectators, who are expected to remain silent during play, not to express vocal disapproval of official decisions, and to applaud losers who have made a good try.

While a tennis player is expected to be merciless and to do his utmost to win every point, he is not supposed to take advantage of an opponent. If some outside interference disrupts an opponent's shot, the player is expected to offer to let him play it over, which the opponent — out of courtesy — will usually politely decline to do. In making a close call on a shot by an opponent, a player is expected to give the opponent the benfit of the doubt and make the call in his favor.

A player never makes disparaging remarks about an opponent's or partner's (in doubles) shots, but he usually verbally applauds their good shots. Tennis is a game of quiet concentration and shouts and yells are as out of place on the court as they would be at a chess match. Displays of temper over a missed shot are equally out of place.

Do not call shots on the opponent's side of the net unless you are specifically asked to. After all, he is closer to the call than you are and while he may make some mistakes, so, probably, will you — and it will all average out. If you strongly suspect an opponent of making bad calls in his own favor, do not play with him again.

In tournament play, a player is not ever expected to question a linesman's calls by voice, look, or in any other manner. Of late, there have come along a few players who express disapproval of official decisions, but such players are not exactly the most popular with the spectators, or their fellow contestants.

GETTING IN SHAPE

Tennis itself is conducive to physical fitness. The courts are full of overweight men and women fighting the war against weight — and winning.

Everything else being equal, the winning player is the one in the best physical condition. There is not an ounce of flab in the entire field of entries in a major tournament and it is unusual to see flaccid muscles or excess weight on those who play tennis regularly.

Australia, a continent with only a million or so more people than the New York metropolitan area, has dominated international tennis for many years — or come close to it. The Australians themselves will tell you that their preeminence in the game is largely due to the great stress they place on conditioning the body for tennis.

It cannot be expected that the novice player will plunge immediately into a program of intensive gymnasium workouts and the double knee jumps that are part of the traditional Australian training routine. (The double knee jump is a leap into the air from a standing position, at the highest point of which both knees are bent and clasped to the chest; this is repeated immediately for as long as

Australian ace
Ken Rosewall
is the epitome
of physical fitness.

the victim can endure, and some Australians have achieved almost 100 in succession.)

What the novice can do is to strengthen his weak points. Weak hands and wrists can be made strong by carrying a semihard rubber ball or one of the devices made specifically for the purpose, and squeezing it at every possible opportunity.

Legs are perhaps the tennis player's most important pieces of physical equipment. Nothing strengthens underpinning like jogging or distance running, with brief sprints. These forms of exercise also develop the lung power a good tennis player requires.

The childhood pastime of skipping rope is fine for the legs and it helps develop speed afoot for tennis. Bending and waist-twisting exercises to strengthen the stomach muscles are also excellent for tennis players, although the game itself tightens up the bands that bind the midsection and prevent paunch.

However, too much gymnasium work and too many exercise routines can dampen a novice's enthusiasm for tennis. Perhaps, in the final analysis, the best way to build up the body for tennis is to play the game itself and practice in those departments of the game in which you are weakest. This not only allows tennis to bring you the peak of physical fitness, it will make your game stronger where you tend to be weakest and improve your playing all around.

SOME TENNIS TIPS AND FACTS

● A beginner should always try to play with someone who is better than he is. It is not generally considered good form to ask a much better player to play with you, but good friends will not mind, and playing "over your head" can have a most beneficial effect on your game, especially if the better player is helpful with suggestions and hints.

● If the handle of your racket tends to become slippery from perspiration, have the grips reversed in order to put the rough side out.

● Cement and wood courts offer fast surfaces, which cause the ball to bounce low. This type of court favors the hard hitter. Grass courts also are relatively fast.

● Clay courts, and those of some compositions, present a comparatively slow surface, which causes the ball to bounce high. These types of courts are favored by sure, steady players rather than the sluggers.

● In doubles, it is wise for the teammate with the stronger backhand to receive in the ad court (where shots usually will be played to his left). The player with the better forehand, of course, is more useful in the deuce court.

● A player should not practice more than one or two strokes in any single session. He should concentrate on these intensely, but cease practice on any single stroke before it becomes monotonous.

SOME GREATS OF TENNIS

It is only necessary to turn to the roster of great players to be convinced that tennis is everybody's game. The long list is studded with the names of players of different backgrounds, abilities, characters, and temperaments, not to mention glamour and crowd appeal.

Any array of tennis hall of famers must be headed by Bill Tilden, Suzanne Lenglen, and Helen Wills Moody, all of whom dominated the game in the Golden Age of Sports in the 1920s and, in the case of Tilden and Mrs. Moody, even beyond.

William Tatem ("Big Bill") Tilden, a Philadelphian, had everything — and in large quantities. While he excelled in every phase of the game, it was his service that was most spectacular. It really deserved the name of cannonball. From his towering height, he shot the ball across the net with a power and speed that was dazzling. If an opponent succeeded in returning a blistering Tilden serve, he was still in trouble because Big Bill could cope with every situation. He was a superb tactician, and had the shots to do almost exactly as he wished on the court.

So consummate was Tilden's skill and command of the sport that in 1925 he won fifty-seven consecutive games in two tournaments in the United States. So great was his determination and courage that in 1921 at Wimbledon he beat B.I.C. Norton 4–6, 2–6, 6–1, 6–0, and 7–5 after Norton had reached match point twice in the final set. In 1922, Tilden had to have part of a finger removed, but he adjusted his grip and continued to play even more brilliantly than before.

Tilden won the U. S. Singles Championship every year from 1920 through 1925, then came back to win it again in 1929 at the age of thirty-six. The following year he again won the Wimbledon singles title, which he had held in 1920 and 1921. He was ranked number one tennis player in the world from 1920 through 1925.

Tilden was a superb showman, playing with an insouciance that belied his great command of the game. His appearance on the court in one of the fuzzy sweaters he called his grizzlies attracted such crowds that when he and Suzanne Lenglen appeared on the scene the old Wimbledon was no longer large enough to accommodate the spectators and in 1922 the new premises of the All England Club were opened by King George V.

An intellectual, Tilden wrote books and plays and was better than fair as an actor. He turned professional in 1931 and was still playing good tennis until shortly before his death in 1953.

Suzanne Lenglen was the personification of sparkle and charisma on the court and, at her peak, was one of the finest women players the game ever has known. She had a devastating smash, was a great volleyer, and, as one sports writer put it, "was everywhere on the court at once." Added to all that, she was extremely accurate and sent a minimum of shots out of the court.

She won the first post-World War I singles championship at Wimbledon in 1919 by beating Mrs. Lambert Chambers after being match points down. She was twenty-two at the time and from that time until 1926, she lost only one singles match. That happened in 1921 when she resigned to Mrs. Molla Mallory, who held the American singles championship in 1915, 1916, 1918, 1920, 1921, 1922, and 1926. Down 2–6 in the first set of the American singles championship, Miss Lenglen withdrew because of illness. Yet she went through the singles of tournaments without losing a game five times in her career.

Suzanne Lenglen electrified the women's game in more ways than one. She created a sensation by appearing on court in a short-sleeved, one-piece dress, wearing lipstick but no petticoat. Before long other women were adopting her sensible garb and the bandeau that was part of her trademark.

Born in Compiegne, France, Miss Lenglen — who turned professional in 1926 — died at the age of thirty-nine of pernicious aenemia, a woman who created her own legend in her own lifetime.

Helen Wills Moody, the attractive girl from Berkeley, California, was so deadly unemotional in play that she became known as "Little Poker Face." She could annihilate an opponent with an overhead smash or lose a set point without giving any outward sign that it meant a thing to her.

During her reign as queen of the courts, Mrs. Moody was virtually unbeatable. Between 1927 and 1932 she won the Wimbledon championship five times, took four U.S. championships, and was champion of France four times. In addition, she won twelve rubbers in Wightman Cup competition. All this she accomplished *without losing a single set.* She was ranked number one among women players in 1927, 1933, 1935, and 1936. She retired from

Left: he had everything.
In one of the toughest of sports,
William ("Big Bill") Tilden,
American ace par excellence,
stayed around the top of
the game for thirty years.

Right: French tennis star
Suzanne Lenglen. She, and
male colleagues such as
René Lacoste, Jean Borota,
and Henri Cochet, dominated
the game in the 1920s.

So unemotional was the American woman ace Helen Wills Moody that she became known as "Little Poker Face."

Fred Perry, England's greatest tennis star, is shown here in dramatic action.

the game in 1938 at the age of thirty-three, while still at, or close to, the peak of her game.

There have been so many other truly great players that it would be almost impossible to list them all. For example, there was Little Bill Johnston, the perennial runner-up to Tilden, who might have dominated the game had not Big Bill been in competition. Fred Perry, Britain's greatest player, certainly belongs on the list for leading his country to Davis Cup triumph from 1933 to 1936 and winning the Wimbledon singles three years in succession, the first to do so after World War I. Californian Ellsworth Vines's sizzling service, deadly forehand, control, and complete command of the game certainly have earned him a place on the roster.

The Four Musketeers must be named if only for the color and excitement they brought to tennis in the 1920s. If for no other reason, the French team of Jean Borota, the "Bounding Basque;" Henri Cochet; Jacques Brugnon; and René Lacoste deserve a place for winning the Davis Cup for France in 1927, despite the presence of Tilden and Johnston on the American team.

Doris Hart, the little girl from St. Louis who started playing tennis at the age of six to forestall a disease that threatened to cripple her, must also be on the list. So must Rod Laver, the Australian left-hander with the destructive backhand; Maureen ("Little Mo") Connolly; Helen Jacobs; Pancho Gonzales; and Arthur Ashe, the first black to win the U.S. men's singles title. Nor can such veterans as Margaret Court or Ken Rosewall be absent from such a list of tennis greats.

Indeed, the list is long and growing ever longer. Certainly from latter-day players like the U.S. Army's methodical Stan Smith, mercurial Ilie Nastase of Rumania, two-handed Chris Evert of California, Australian aborigine Yvonne Goolagong, Billie Jean King, and others will come more than a few who will occupy much-deserved niches in the tennis hall of fame.

Top left: photographed at Wimbledon in 1952 are four women aces.
Left to right are Shirley Fry and Doris Hart. They retained their title in the
women's doubles by defeating Louise Brough (third from left) and Maureen
("Little Mo") Connolly. Top right: American woman star Helen Jacobs returns
a shot at Forest Hills in the 1930s. Bottom right: making a forehand return is
Pancho Gonzales, one of the most durable tennis pros of all time. Bottom left:
the agile Arthur Ashe saves one in the backcourt.

Top left: Chris Evert
exhibits her
two-handed back-
hand. Top right:
Australia's brilliant
challenger Yvonne
Goolagong. Left:
Margaret Smith Court,
strokes back a fore-
hand shot in tourna-
ment play.

GLOSSARY

Ace – A fair service that the receiver does not touch with his racket.

Advantage or Ad – When one player has scored point after the game has been tied at *deuce* he is said to have the advantage. The score is announced "advantage in" if the server wins the point, "advantage out" if it is won by the receiver.

Ad Court – Service court on receiver's left. Also called *backhand court* and *second court*.

Alley – Two lanes bordering the singles sidelines and used as boundaries only for doubles.

Approach Shot – A shot hit deep into an opponent's court to enable the stroker to follow it to the net for a volley.

Backcourt – That area of the court behind the rear service lines.

Backhand – Stroke made on left side of the body by right-handers, right side by left-handers.

Backhand Court – See *ad court*.

Backspin – Spin given the ball by hitting it with a downward motion.

Baselines – Lines at each end of the court.

Bevel – Diagonal side of racket handle.

Center Mark – Line on or near baseline that divides the line into equal halves for serving.

Center Service Line – Line separating two service courts.

Deuce – Score (instead of 40 — all) when both sides have won three points, or when the player with the *advantage* loses the next point. Also, a set in which both sides have won at least five games.

Deuce Court – Service court on receiver's right. Also called *first court*.

Doubles – Game played with teams of two on each side of the court.

Drive – Stroke hit with full sideward swing after ball has bounced. Also called *groundstroke*.

Drop Shot – A soft shot hit with backspin to make the ball drop close to the net.

Error – A return that is missed completely, hit after the second bounce, goes out, or goes into the net.

Fault – A serve that does not land in proper service court or a serve illegally struck, as a *foot fault*.

First Court – See *deuce court*.

Foot Fault – Improper position of feet when serving. Counted as a point against the server even though the serve lands in the proper service court.

Forecourt – Area of the court in front of the service line.

Forehand – Stroke made on right side of body by right-handers, vice versa by left-handers.

Groundstroke – See *drive*.

Half-Volley — Stroke made just as ball bounces from surface of court.

Head – That part of the racket which is strung.

Let – Ball that hits net on serve and drops into proper service court. It must be served over. Also called *let serve*.

Let Point – A point that for any reason must be played over.

Let Serve – See *let*.

Lob – A high, lofted ball.

Overhead – See *smash*.

Overspin – See *topspin*.

Placement – Shot that lands fair but out of reach of opponent.

Rally – Hitting the ball back and forth during play or practice. Also used as a noun to describe a prolonged exchange.

Receiver – Player who receives the serve.

Second Court – See *ad court*.

Serve or Service – Stroke that puts the ball into play at the beginning of each point.

Service Court – Courts between the net and service line on each side of the net into which the ball must be served.

Service Line – Line running parallel to the net and baselines that bounds the rear of the service courts.

Sidelines – Lines on the sides of the court that bound the playing area.

Sidespin – Spin imparted by bringing the racket across the ball sidewise.

Singles – Tennis played with one player on each side.

Smash – Stroke in which a lofted ball is hit very hard. Sometimes called *overhead*.

Throat – That part of the racket which connects the head to the handle.

Topspin – Spin imparted by bringing the racket over the top of the ball. Also called *overspin*.

Volley – A shot in which ball is hit before it strikes the surface of the court. Also used as a verb.

INDEX

DATE DUE